# by Iain Gray

LangSyne

PUBLISHING

WRITING *to* REMEMBER

## Lang**Syne**

**PUBLISHING**

WRITING *to* REMEMBER

E-mail: info@lang-syne.co.uk

Distributed in the Republic of Ireland by Portfolio Group,
Kilbarrack Ind. Est. Kilbarrack, Dublin 5.
T:00353(01) 839 4918 F:00353(01) 839 5826
sales@portfoliogroup.ie
www.portfoliogroup.ie

Design by Dorothy Meikle
Printed by Ricoh Print Scotland

© Lang Syne Publishers Ltd 2012

ISBN 978-1-85217-248-0

# Doherty

**MOTTO:**
Our heritage
(and) For my inheritance.

**CREST:**
A hand grasping a scimitar.

**NAME** variations include:
Ó Dochartaigh *(Gaelic)*
O'Doherty
Docharty
Docherty
Dogherty
Dougharty
Dougherty

*Chapter one:*
# Origins of Irish surnames

**According to an old saying, there are two types of Irish –
those who actually are Irish and those who wish they were.**

This sentiment is only one example of the allure that the
high romance and drama of the proud nation's history holds
for thousands of people scattered across the world today.

It's a sad fact, however, that the vast majority of Irish
surnames are found far beyond Irish shores, rather than on
the Emerald Isle itself.

The population stood at around eight million souls in
1841, but today it stands at fewer than six million.

This is mainly a tragic consequence of the potato
famine, also known as the Great Hunger, which devastated
Ireland between 1845 and 1849.

The Irish peasantry had become almost wholly reliant
for basic sustenance on the potato, first introduced from the
Americas in the seventeenth century.

When the crop was hit by a blight, at least 800,000
people starved to death while an estimated two million
others were forced to seek a new life far from their native
shores – particularly in America, Canada, and Australia.

The effects of the potato blight continued until about
1851, by which time a firm pattern of emigration had
become established.

Ireland's loss, however, was to the gain of the countries in which the immigrants settled, contributing enormously, as their descendants do today, to the well being of the nations in which their forefathers settled.

But those who were forced through dire circumstance to establish a new life in foreign parts never forgot their roots, or the proud heritage and traditions of the land that gave them birth.

Nor do their descendants.

It is a heritage that is inextricably bound up in the colourful variety of Irish names themselves – and the origin and history of these names forms an integral part of the vibrant drama that is the nation's history, one of both glorious fortune and tragic misfortune.

This history is well documented, and one of the most important and fascinating of the earliest sources are *The Annals of the Four Masters*, compiled between 1632 and 1636 by four friars at the Franciscan Monastery in County Donegal.

Compiled from earlier sources, and purporting to go back to the Biblical Deluge, much of the material takes in the mythological origins and history of Ireland and the Irish.

This includes tales of successive waves of invaders and settlers such as the Fomorians, the Partholonians, the Nemedians, the Fir Bolgs, the Tuatha De Danann, and the Laigain.

Of particular interest are the *Milesian Genealogies*,

because the majority of Irish clans today claim a descent from either Heremon, Ir, or Heber – three of the sons of Milesius, a king of what is now modern day Spain.

These sons invaded Ireland in the second millennium B.C, apparently in fulfilment of a mysterious prophecy received by their father.

This Milesian lineage is said to have ruled Ireland for nearly 3,000 years, until the island came under the sway of England's King Henry II in 1171 following what is known as the Cambro-Norman invasion.

This is an important date not only in Irish history in general, but for the effect the invasion subsequently had for Irish surnames.

'Cambro' comes from the Welsh, and 'Cambro-Norman' describes those Welsh knights of Norman origin who invaded Ireland.

But they were invaders who stayed, inter-marrying with the native Irish population and founding their own proud dynasties that bore Cambro-Norman names such as Archer, Barbour, Brannagh, Fitzgerald, Fitzgibbon, Fleming, Joyce, Plunkett, and Walsh – to name only a few.

These 'Cambro-Norman' surnames that still flourish throughout the world today form one of the three main categories in which Irish names can be placed – those of Gaelic-Irish, Cambro-Norman, and Anglo-Irish.

Previous to the Cambro-Norman invasion of the twelfth century, and throughout the earlier invasions and settlement of those wild bands of sea rovers known as the Vikings in the eighth and ninth centuries, the population of the island was relatively small, and it was normal for a person to be identified through the use of only a forename.

But as population gradually increased and there were many more people with the same forename, surnames were adopted to distinguish one person, or one community, from another.

Individuals identified themselves with their own particular tribe, or 'tuath', and this tribe – that also became known as a clann, or clan – took its name from some distinguished ancestor who had founded the clan.

The Gaelic-Irish form of the name Kelly, for example, is Ó Ceallaigh, or O'Kelly, indicating descent from an original 'Ceallaigh', with the 'O' denoting 'grandson of.' The name was later anglicised to Kelly.

The prefix 'Mac' or 'Mc', meanwhile, as with the clans of the Scottish Highlands, denotes 'son of.'

Although the Irish clans had much in common with their Scottish counterparts, one important difference lies in what are known as 'septs', or branches, of the clan.

Septs of Scottish clans were groups who often bore an entirely different name from the clan name but were under the clan's protection.

In Ireland, septs were groups that shared the same name and who could be found scattered throughout the four provinces of Ulster, Leinster, Munster, and Connacht.

The 'golden age' of the Gaelic-Irish clans, infused as their veins were with the blood of Celts, pre-dates the Viking invasions of the eighth and ninth centuries and the Norman invasion of the twelfth century, and the sacred heart of the country was the Hill of Tara, near the River Boyne, in County Meath.

Known in Gaelic as 'Teamhar na Rí', or Hill of Kings, it was the royal seat of the 'Ard Rí Éireann', or High King of Ireland, to whom the petty kings, or chieftains, from the island's provinces were ultimately subordinate.

It was on the Hill of Tara, beside a stone pillar known as the Irish 'Lia Fáil', or Stone of Destiny, that the High Kings were inaugurated and, according to legend, this stone would emit a piercing screech that could be heard all over Ireland when touched by the hand of the rightful king.

The Hill of Tara is today one of the island's main tourist attractions.

Opposition to English rule over Ireland, established in the wake of the Cambro-Norman invasion, broke out frequently and the harsh solution adopted by the powerful forces of the Crown was to forcibly evict the native Irish from their lands.

These lands were then granted to Protestant colonists, or 'planters', from Britain.

Many of these colonists, ironically, came from Scotland and were the descendants of the original 'Scotti', or 'Scots', who gave their name to Scotland after migrating there in the fifth century A.D., from the north of Ireland.

Colonisation entailed harsh penal laws being imposed on the majority of the native Irish population, stripping them practically of all of their rights.

The Crown's main bastion in Ireland was Dublin and its environs, known as the Pale, and it was the dispossessed peasantry who lived outside this Pale, desperately striving to eke out a meagre living.

It was this that gave rise to the modern-day expression of someone or something being 'beyond the pale'.

Attempts were made to stamp out all aspects of the ancient Gaelic-Irish culture, to the extent that even to bear a Gaelic-Irish name was to invite discrimination.

This is why many Gaelic-Irish names were anglicised with, for example, and noted above, Ó Ceallaigh, or O'Kelly, being anglicised to Kelly.

Succeeding centuries have seen strong revivals of Gaelic-Irish consciousness, however, and this has led to many families reverting back to the original form of their name, while the language itself is frequently found on the fluent tongues of an estimated 90,000 to 145,000 of the island's population.

Ireland's turbulent history of religious and political strife is one that lasted well into the twentieth century, a landmark century that saw the partition of the island into the twenty-six counties of the independent Republic of

Ireland, or Eire, and the six counties of Northern Ireland, or Ulster.

Dublin, originally founded by Vikings, is now a vibrant and truly cosmopolitan city while the proud city of Belfast is one of the jewels in the crown of Ulster.

It was Saint Patrick who first brought the light of Christianity to Ireland in the fifth century A.D.

Interpretations of this Christian message have varied over the centuries, often leading to bitter sectarian conflict – but the many intricately sculpted Celtic Crosses found all over the island are symbolic of a unity that crosses the sectarian divide.

It is an image that fuses the 'old gods' of the Celts with Christianity.

All the signs from the early years of this new millennium indicate that sectarian strife may soon become a thing of the past – with the Irish and their many kinsfolk across the world, be they Protestant or Catholic, finding common purpose in the rich tapestry of their shared heritage.

*Chapter two:*
# The warrior king

**Bearers of the proud surname of Doherty, in all its rich
variety of spellings, can lay claim to what is believed to
be one of the oldest hereditary surnames in Europe.**

In Gaelic, its form is Ó Dochartaigh, thought to have
meant 'obstructive' – a rather apt designation considering
the tenacity with which generations of bearers of the name
defended their ancient rights and privileges in the face of
aggression.

The genealogy of the Dohertys of today is truly
illustrious, stretching back as it does through the mists of
time to some of Ireland's most celebrated heroes.

The Doherty name stems from Dochartach, who was
twelfth in lineal descent from Conall Gulban.

Conall, in turn, was one of the sons of Niall
Noíghiallach, better known to posterity as the great warrior
king Niall of the Nine Hostages.

The dramatic life and times of this ancestor of the
Dohertys are steeped in stirring Celtic myth and legend.

The youngest son of Eochaidh Mugmedon, king of the
province of Connacht, his mother died in childbirth and he
was brought up by his evil stepmother Mongfhinn who, for
reasons best known to herself, was determined that he
should die.

She accordingly abandoned him naked on the Hill of Tara, inauguration site of the Ard Rí, or High Kings, of Ireland, but he was found by a wandering bard who took him back to his father.

One legend is that Mongfhinn sent Niall and his four brothers – Brian, Fiachra, Ailill, and Fergus – to a renowned prophet who was also a blacksmith to determine which of them would succeed their father as Ard Rí.

The blacksmith, known as Sitchin, set the lads a task by deliberately setting fire to his forge.

Niall's brothers ran in and came out carrying the spear-heads, fuel, hammers, and barrels of beer that they had rescued, but Niall staggered out clutching the heavy anvil so vital to the blacksmith's trade.

By this deed, Sitchin prophesied that Niall would be the one who would take on the glorious mantle of kingship.

Another prophetic incident occurred one day while Niall and his brothers were engaged in the hunt.

Thirsty from their efforts they encountered an ugly old woman who offered them water – but only in return for a kiss.

Three of the lads, no doubt repelled by her green teeth and scaly skin, refused. Fiachra pecked her lightly on the cheek and, by this act, she prophesied that he would one day reign at Tara – but only briefly.

The bold Niall, however, kissed her fully on the lips. The hag then demanded that he should now have full sexual intercourse with her and, undaunted, he did so.

Through this action she was suddenly transformed into a stunningly beautiful young woman known as Flaithius, or Royalty, who predicted that he would become the greatest High King of Ireland.

His stepmother Mongfhinn later tried to poison him, but accidentally took the deadly potion herself and died.

This legend relates to what was known as the Festival of Mongfhinn, or Feis na Samhan (the Fest of Samhain), because it was on the evening of October 31, on Samhain's Eve, that the poisoning incident is said to have taken place.

It was believed for centuries in Ireland that, on Samhain Eve, Mongfhinn's warped and wicked spirit would roam the land in hungry search of children's souls.

The Festival, or Feast, of Samhain, is today better known as Halloween.

Niall became Ard Rí in 379 A.D. and embarked on the series of military campaigns and other daring adventures that would subsequently earn him the title of Niall of the Nine Hostages.

The nine countries and territories into which he raided and took hostages for ransom were the Irish provinces of Munster, Leinster, Connacht, and Ulster, Britain, and the territories of the Saxons, Morini, Picts, and Dalriads.

Niall's most famous hostage was a young lad known as Succat, son of Calpernius, a Romano-Briton who lived in the area of present day Milford Haven, on the Welsh coast.

Later known as Patricius, or Patrick, he became renowned as Ireland's patron saint, St. Patrick, responsible for bringing the light of Christianity to the island in the early years of the fifth century A.D.

Raiding in Gaul, in the area of Boulogne-sur-mer in present day France, Niall was ambushed and killed by one of his treacherous subjects in 405 A.D.

But his legacy survived through the royal dynasties and clans founded by his sons – not least Conall Gulban, who laid the foundations of the Doherty dynasty that became centred in Inishowen, in present day Co. Donegal in the northwest of Ireland.

It was here that for centuries the Dohertys ruled as Lords of Inishowen and the remains of one of their impressive castles, built about 1430, can be seen to this day at Buncrana, between Lough Foyle and Lough Swilly.

What would subsequently prove to be the event that sowed the seeds of the destruction of the ancient Gaelic way of life of proud native Irish clans such as the Dohertys came in the late twelfth century – with the Cambro-Norman invasion and the subsequent consolidation of the power of the English Crown over the island.

Twelfth century Ireland was far from being a unified nation, split up as it was into territories ruled over by squabbling chieftains such as Dermot MacMurrough, who ruled as kings in their own right – and this inter-clan rivalry worked to the advantage of the invaders.

In a series of bloody conflicts one chieftain, or king, would occasionally gain the upper hand over his rivals, and by 1156 the most powerful was Muirchertach MacLochlainn, king of the powerful O'Neills.

He was opposed by the equally powerful Rory O'Connor, king of the province of Connacht, but he increased his power and influence by allying himself with Dermot MacMurrough, king of Leinster.

MacLochlainn and MacMurrough were aware that the main key to the kingdom of Ireland was the thriving trading port of Dublin that had been established by invading Vikings, or Ostmen, in 852 A.D.

Dublin was taken by the combined forces of the Leinster and Connacht kings, but when MacLochlainn died the Dubliners rose up in revolt and overthrew the unpopular MacMurrough.

A triumphant Rory O'Connor entered Dublin and was later inaugurated as Ard Rí, but the proud Dermott MacMurrough was not one to humbly accept defeat.

He appealed for help from England's Henry II in unseating O'Connor – an act that was to radically affect the future course of Ireland's fortunes in general and those of the Dohertys and other native Irish clans in particular.

*Chapter three:*

# Resistance and rebellion

**Henry II agreed to help MacMurrough, but distanced himself from direct action by delegating his Norman subjects in Wales with the task.**

These ambitious and battle-hardened barons and knights had first settled in Wales following the Norman Conquest of England in 1066 and, with an eye on rich booty, plunder, and lands, were only too eager to obey their sovereign's wishes and furnish aid to MacMurrough.

MacMurrough crossed the Irish Sea to Bristol, where he rallied powerful barons such as Robert Fitzstephen and Maurice Fitzgerald to his cause, along with Gilbert de Clare, Earl of Pembroke, and also known as Strongbow.

The mighty Norman war machine soon moved into action, and so fierce and disciplined was their onslaught on the forces of Rory O'Connor and his allies that by 1171 they had re-captured Dublin, in the name of MacMurrough, and other strategically important territories.

It was now that a nervous Henry II began to take cold feet over the venture, realising that he may have created a rival in the form of a separate Norman kingdom in Ireland.

Accordingly, he landed on the island, near Waterford, at the head of a large army in October of 1171 with the aim of curbing the power of his Cambro-Norman barons.

Protracted war between the king and his barons was averted, however, when the barons submitted to the royal will, promising homage and allegiance in return for holding the territories they had conquered in the king's name.

Henry also received the submission and homage of many of the Irish chieftains – but the Dohertys were resolute in their defiance.

English dominion over Ireland was ratified through the Treaty of Windsor of 1175, under the terms of which Rory O'Connor, for example, was allowed to rule territory unoccupied by the Normans in the role of a vassal of the king.

Ireland groaned under a weight of oppression, directed in the main against native Irish clans such as the Dohertys.

An indication of the harsh treatment meted out to them can be found in a desperate plea sent to Pope John XII by Roderick O'Carroll of Ely, Donald O'Neil of Ulster, and a number of other Irish chieftains in 1318.

They stated: 'As it very constantly happens, whenever an Englishman, by perfidy or craft, kills an Irishman, however noble, or however innocent, be he clergy or layman, there is no penalty or correction enforced against the person who may be guilty of such wicked murder.

'But rather the more eminent the person killed and the higher rank which he holds among his own people, so much more is the murderer honoured and rewarded by the English, and not merely by the people at large, but also by the religious and bishops of the English race.'

This appeal to the Pope had little effect on what became the increasingly harsh policy of the occupying English Crown against the native Irish.

In the complex politics and shifting alliances of the time, native Irish clans such as the Dohertys had to frequently bend like a shamrock in the wind to preserve their best interests.

Often paying only mere lip service to the English Crown, some were granted honours and titles to retain their albeit dubious loyalties – including Shane Mor O'Doherty, who was knighted in 1541 and his son Shane Og O'Doherty, knighted in 1585.

The straw that finally broke the camel's back in relation to the uneasy relationship between the English Crown and the Dohertys, in common with many other prominent Catholic Irish families, proved to be the policy of 'plantation', or settlement of loyal Protestants on land held by native Irish.

This started during the reign from 1491 to 1547 of Henry VIII, whose Reformation effectively outlawed the established Roman Catholic faith throughout his dominions.

This plantation continued throughout the subsequent reigns of Elizabeth I, James I (James VI of Scotland), and in the wake of the devastating Cromwellian invasion of 1649.

Born in 1587 Cahir O'Doherty, son of Shane Og O'Doherty, is arguably one of the most famous bearers of the name.

It was through his disgust with the policy of plantation that he rebelled against the Crown and unwittingly sealed the final doom of his family.

A number of Irish earls had rebelled against the policy of plantation and harsh penal policies against Catholics but, following their defeat at the battle of Kinsale in 1601 and the final suppression of the rebellion three years later in Ulster, their future existence hung by a precarious thread.

Three years later, in September of 1607 and in what is known as The Flight of the Earls, Hugh O'Neill, 2nd Earl of Tyrone and Rory O'Donnell, 1st Earl of Tyrconnel, sailed into foreign exile from the village of Rathmullan, on the shore of Lough Swilly, in the Doherty homeland of Co. Donegal, accompanied by ninety loyal followers.

Cahir O'Doherty had meanwhile been knighted for his military service to the English Crown and appointed admiral of the city of Derry.

In the turbulent politics of the time he was accused of treason and, described as 'that most audacious traitor', he decided to rebel against the policy of plantation by attacking and burning Derry and killing its Crown-appointed governor.

The Crown's vengeance for what is known as O'Doherty's' Rebellion was swift: Cahir O'Doherty was killed and his head lopped off and sent off in triumph for display in Dublin as a dire warning to others.

The failed rebellion not only served to further consolidate the English Crown's tenacious grip on Ireland and further the policy of plantation, but also to smash the once proud power and influence of the Dohertys forever.

Bloodied but unbeaten, succeeding generations of

Dohertys would however continue the struggle for not only their nation's freedom and independence but also the rights of the ordinary man and woman.

Not least among them was Kevin Izard O'Doherty, born in 1823 and who, as a medical student in Dublin and a member of the Young Irelander movement, wrote a number of celebrated articles advocating Home Rule.

Tried for treason, he was transported to present day Tasmania but later returned to Dublin.

Returning in 1862 to Brisbane, Australia, after completing his interrupted medical studies, he not only founded a successful medical practice but also became a prominent member of the Queensland Legislative Assembly.

With his heart always in Ireland, however, he returned to his native land more than twenty years later and was greeted with such acclaim that he was elected as the Member of Parliament for North Meath.

Returning to Australia three years later, he found that the medical practice he had set up no longer existed and he died, in poverty, in 1905.

Recognised as a leading figure in the formation of what became the organisation for workers' rights known as the British trades union movement, John Doherty was born in the Doherty homeland of Inishowen, Co. Donegal, in 1798.

Moving from Ireland and finding work in the harsh environment of the sweat shops of the Manchester textile works, in England, in 1816, he was sentenced to two years hard labour two years later on trumped-up charges of assault while striking for higher wages.

By 1828 he was instrumental in the formation of the Society for the Protection of Children Employed in Cotton Factories and shortly after that was the main driving force behind the Grand General Union of Operative Spinners of the United Kingdom.

This was followed by the formation of the General Union of Trades and later the National Association for the Protection of Labour.

In parallel with his trades union activities Doherty also published his own newspaper, *Voice of the People*. The radical views espoused in the newspaper led to him being imprisoned again for a time in 1832.

Undaunted, he continued his campaign for much needed social reform until his death in 1854.

In contemporary times it was recorded in the *Derry Journal* newspaper of March 9, 2007 how up to 400,000 records of the Dohertys were unfortunately destroyed in what was thought to have been an electrical fire at the clan's family history centre in Buncrana, Co. Donegal.

Professor Pat O'Dougherty, formerly of Oakland University, Michigan, and who moved to Donegal in 1984, had carefully compiled the records over the past forty years.

Much of what was lost in the blaze relates to records of Dohertys in Canada, the United States, and Australia – but it is hoped that much of this may be retrieved from records that had been backed up on computer.

*Chapter four:*

# On the world stage

**Generations of Dohertys have enjoyed celebrity through their involvement in a diverse range of callings and pursuits – in all the different varieties of the spelling of the surname.**

In the world of popular music, **Pete Doherty**, born in Northumberland, England, in 1979, and formerly of the band The Libertines, is the controversial singer with the band Babyshambles and a sometimes partner of supermodel Kate Moss.

Born in Halifax, Nova Scotia, in 1940, **Denny Doherty** was the Canadian singer and songwriter who, along with Cass Elliot, John Phillips, and Michelle Phillips, was a founding member of the hugely successful 1960s band The Mamas and the Papas.

The early and truly gruelling financial struggles of the newly formed band on America's west coast are famously recorded on *Creeque Alley*, which, along with *California Dreaming* and other songs became one of their many hits.

It contains the line 'John and Denny, working for a penny …'

Denny Doherty died in Mississauga, Ontario, in January of 2007.

On the stage, **Shannon Doherty**, born in 1971 in

Memphis, Tennessee, is the American actress whose first major role was as Jenny Wilder in the *Little House on the Prairie* television series; she has since starred in the *Beverley Hills 90210* television series and as Prue Halliwell in the *Charmed* series.

In the world of art, **Willie Doherty**, born in Derry, Northern Ireland, in 1959, is the Irish artist who specialises mainly in photography and video; he was short listed for the much sought after Turner Prize in both 1994 and 2003.

Still in the world of art, **William O'Doherty**, born in Dublin in 1835 and who died in 1860, trained in painting in the studios of the Royal Dublin Society before turning his talents to sculpture; by 1857 his sculptures were greeted with such acclaim that they were exhibited in London's prestigious Royal Academy.

In the world of books, Paul C. Doherty, better known as **P.C. Doherty**, is the highly successful international author who also, rather confusingly, writes under the pen names of Anna Apostolu, Michael Clynes, Ann Dukthas, C.L. Grace, Vanessa Alexander, and Paul Harding.

Born in Middlesbrough, England, in 1946, and the recipient of a doctorate in history from the University of Oxford, his specialism is historical mysteries and novels, including the *Hugh Corbett Medieval Mysteries*, the *Canterbury Tales of Mystery and Murder*, and *The Sorrowful Mysteries of Brother Athelstan*.

In addition to his career as a novelist, he is also the

headmaster of a Roman Catholic High School in England.

Northern Ireland-born **Richard Doherty** is a prolific military historian whose intensively researched books on both Irish history in particular and British history in general include *The Williamite War in Ireland 1688-1691*, *Irish Men and Women in the Second World War*, and *The History of the Eighth Army, 1941 to 1945*.

More controversially, Canadian-based **Earl Doherty** is the best-selling author of the 1999 *The Jesus Puzzle*, a book that argues Jesus Christ should not be seen as a real historical character but rather as a mythological figure, albeit a heroic one.

In the competitive world of sport, **Matt Doherty**, born in Long Island in 1962, is the celebrated American basketball coach who is renowned for his career from 2000 to 2003 as head coach at North Carolina.

At the time of writing he is head coach at Southern Methodist University, following a stint as head coach at Florida Atlantic University.

Known variously as 'The Darlin' of Dublin', 'Ken-do', and 'Krafty Ken', **Ken Doherty**, born in Dublin in 1969, is the Irish professional snooker player who is the only player ever to have held the titles of world amateur and world professional champion.

The first title was gained in 1989, while the second was achieved in 1997; at the time of writing he is ranked fourth in the snooker world rankings.

On the tennis court, **Laurence Doherty**, born in 1875, was the English tennis player who was Wimbledon Singles Champion for four years in succession from 1902.

He was also Doubles Champion on seven occasions, U.S Singles Champion in 1903 and U.S. Doubles Champion in both 1902 and 1903.

His older brother, **Reggie Doherty**, was also a talented tennis player.

In athletics, **John Doherty**, born in 1905 and who died in 1996, was the American athlete who won a bronze medal in the Decathlon event at the 1928 Olympics in Amsterdam.

A number of Dohertys have also excelled on the football pitch.

Nicknamed 'Peter the Great', **Peter Doherty**, born in 1913 in Magherafelt, Co. Londonderry, was the Northern Ireland footballer whose playing career began with Glentoran, in the Irish League.

He later played for a number of English clubs, including Blackpool, Manchester City, and Derby County. Capped sixteen times for the Northern Ireland national team, he later managed it and led it to the finals of the 1958 World Cup.

Doherty, who died in 1990, was inducted into the English Football Hall of Fame in 2002.

Known as 'The Doc', or 'Ginger Pele', **Gary Doherty**, born in 1981 in Carndonagh, Co. Donegal, is the Irish football defender who, at the time of writing, plays for Norwich City.

Still on the football pitch, Thomas Henderson Docherty, born in Glasgow in 1928, and better known as **Tommy Docherty**, or 'the Doc' is the former professional football player and manager who started his playing career with Shettleston Juniors in 1946.

After being demobilised from National Service, during which he played football for the British Army, he was signed to Glasgow Celtic Football Club.

A career as player with a variety of other clubs such as Preston North End, Arsenal, Chelsea, Queen's Park Rangers, Aston Villa, and Hull followed in rapid succession over a number of years that also saw him honoured with twenty-five full Scotland International Caps.

'The Doc' also enjoyed a managerial career with a number of clubs, including Australia's Sydney Olympic and South Melbourne clubs, before finally 'retiring' from the game in 1988.

He has since pursued a successful career as a football pundit and popular after-dinner speaker.

From the sporting arena to the world of medical research, **Professor Peter C. Doherty**, born in Brisbane, Queensland, in 1940, is the Australian veterinary surgeon and researcher who, in 1996, was a co-recipient of the Nobel Prize in Physiology or Medicine.

Also in the sciences, **John Doherty**, born in 1688 and who lived for most of his life in Worcester, England, was a noted mathematician.

Dohertys have also been eminent in the legal profession.

Born in Montreal in 1855, **Charles Doherty** was the lawyer and Minister of Justice who represented Canada at the League of Nations at Versailles, France, in 1919, while John Doherty, born in 1783, was a celebrated Chief Justice of Ireland.

Born in Nizhny Novgorod, Russia, in 1896, Ekaterina Kolyshkin is better known as **Catherine Doherty**, the social activist and founder of the Madonna House Apostolate that traces its roots back to when she worked among the poor in Toronto.

Fleeing Russia in the wake of the Russian Revolution, she first settled in England but later immigrated to Canada.

By 1936 she had moved to the United States, and it was here that in 1943 she married Edward J. Doherty, better known as **Eddie Doherty**, one of America's most famous newspaper reporters.

Eddie, born in Chicago in 1890, was at one time billed across the nation as America's highest paid reporter, and it was through working on a story concerning Catherine's apostolate work in Harlem, New York, that the couple married.

A year after their marriage his screenplay for the movie *The Sullivans* was nominated for an Academy Award for Best Screenplay.

The couple moved back to Catherine's former base in

Canada in 1947 and established the apostolate on a firmer basis; today, it has more than 200 staff workers and more than 22 missionary field houses across the world.

Eddie Doherty died in 1975, while Catherine died ten years later.

Pope John Paul II opened her cause for canonisation as a saint in 2000, with the granting of the title 'Servant of God' – one of the steps along the road to possible sainthood.

## *Key dates in Ireland's history from the first settlers to the formation of the Irish Republic:*

**circa 7000 B.C.** Arrival and settlement of Stone Age people.

**circa 3000 B.C.** Arrival of settlers of New Stone Age period.

**circa 600 B.C.** First arrival of the Celts.

**200 A.D.** Establishment of Hill of Tara, Co. Meath, as seat of the High Kings.

**circa 432 A.D.** Christian mission of St. Patrick.

**800-920 A.D.** Invasion and subsequent settlement of Vikings.

**1002 A.D.** Brian Boru recognised as High King.

**1014** Brian Boru killed at battle of Clontarf.

**1169-1170** Cambro-Norman invasion of the island.

**1171** Henry II claims Ireland for the English Crown.

**1366** Statutes of Kilkenny ban marriage between native Irish and English.

**1529-1536** England's Henry VIII embarks on religious Reformation.

**1536** Earl of Kildare rebels against the Crown.

**1541** Henry VIII declared King of Ireland.

**1558** Accession to English throne of Elizabeth I.

**1565** Battle of Affane.

**1569-1573** First Desmond Rebellion.

**1579-1583** Second Desmond Rebellion.

**1594-1603** Nine Years War.

**1606** Plantation' of Scottish and English settlers.

| | |
|---|---|
| **1607** | Flight of the Earls. |
| **1632-1636** | Annals of the Four Masters compiled. |
| **1641** | Rebellion over policy of plantation and other grievances. |
| **1649** | Beginning of Cromwellian conquest. |
| **1688** | Flight into exile in France of Catholic Stuart monarch James II as Protestant Prince William of Orange invited to take throne of England along with his wife, Mary. |
| **1689** | William and Mary enthroned as joint monarchs; siege of Derry. |
| **1690** | Jacobite forces of James defeated by William at battle of the Boyne (July) and Dublin taken. |
| **1691** | Athlone taken by William; Jacobite defeats follow at Aughrim, Galway, and Limerick; conflict ends with Treaty of Limerick (October) and Irish officers allowed to leave for France. |
| **1695** | Penal laws introduced to restrict rights of Catholics; banishment of Catholic clergy. |
| **1704** | Laws introduced constricting rights of Catholics in landholding and public office. |
| **1728** | Franchise removed from Catholics. |
| **1791** | Foundation of United Irishmen republican movement. |
| **1796** | French invasion force lands in Bantry Bay. |
| **1798** | Defeat of Rising in Wexford and death of United Irishmen leaders Wolfe Tone and Lord Edward Fitzgerald. |

| | |
|---|---|
| **1800** | Act of Union between England and Ireland. |
| **1803** | Dublin Rising under Robert Emmet. |
| **1829** | Catholics allowed to sit in Parliament. |
| **1845-1849** | The Great Hunger: thousands starve to death as potato crop fails and thousands more emigrate. |
| **1856** | Phoenix Society founded. |
| **1858** | Irish Republican Brotherhood established. |
| **1873** | Foundation of Home Rule League. |
| **1893** | Foundation of Gaelic League. |
| **1904** | Foundation of Irish Reform Association. |
| **1913** | Dublin strikes and lockout. |
| **1916** | Easter Rising in Dublin and proclamation of an Irish Republic. |
| **1917** | Irish Parliament formed after Sinn Fein election victory. |
| **1919-1921** | War between Irish Republican Army and British Army. |
| **1922** | Irish Free State founded, while six northern counties remain part of United Kingdom as Northern Ireland, or Ulster; civil war up until 1923 between rival republican groups. |
| **1949** | Foundation of Irish Republic after all remaining constitutional links with Britain are severed. |